School's Out

Randy Brooks

Other Haiku-Related Publications

In Her Blue Eyes: Jessica Poems. Decatur, Illinois: Brooks Books, 1998.

Black Ant's Journey to Japan: A Modern Tanka Journal. Gualala, California: AHA Online Books, 1998. URL: www.faximum.com/aha.d/blackant.htm

Me Too! Battle Ground, Indiana: High/Coo Press, 1985.

The Last Quarter Mile. Florence, Oregon: Grey Whale Press, 1981.

Barbwire Holds Its Ground. Battle Ground, Indiana: High/Coo Press, 1981.

The Rosebud Bursts. Battle Ground, Indiana: High/Coo Press, 1979.

Where Will Mockingbird Nest? LaCrosse, Wisconsin: Juniper Press, 1977

Co-editor with George Swede, *Global Haiku: 25 Outstanding Poets*. Essex, England: Iron Press, forthcoming.

Editor and Webmaster, "English-Language Haiku Web Site." Decatur, Illinois: Brooks Books, spring 1998. URL: www.family-net.net/~brooksbooks

Co-editor with Lee Gurga, *A Solitary Leaf: Haiku Society of America 1996 Members Anthology*. New York, New York: The Haiku Society of America, 1997.

Co-editor with Lee Gurga, Barbara Ressler, and Harvey Hess, *Fallen Snow: Haiku for Winter*. Cedar Falls, Iowa: Eight Pound Tiger Press, 1996.

Co-Editor with Lee Gurga, *Midwest Haiku Anthology*. Decatur, Illinois: Brooks Books, 1992.

School's Out

Selected *haiku of*
Randy M. Brooks

P r e s s   H e r e
Foster City, California

Press Here
P.O. Box 4014
Foster City, California
94404 USA

ISBN 1-878798-20-0

Photography by Garry Gay

Grateful acknowledgment is made to the editors of the following publications in which some of these poems appeared in present or previous versions: *AHA Online Books, Alchemist, Amoskeag, Bare Bones, Bear Creek Haiku, Big Sky, Black Bough, Brussels Sprout, Centering, Chalk Circle, Cicada* (Canada), *Cicada* (California), *Cream City Review, EPIC News, Frogpond, Gendai Haiku, Grey Whale Press, HAI, Haiku Seasons* (Kodansha, 1996), *Haiku World* (Kodansha, 1996), *The Haiku Handbook* (McGraw-Hill, 1985; Kodansha, 1989), *Haiku Zashi Zo, Heron Quarterly, High/Coo Quarterly, High/Coo Press, Hoshi Haiku, Hyacinths & Biscuits, Hummingbird, Inkstone, Janus-SCTH, Japan Air Lines Anthology* (1988), *Juniper Press, Kusamakura Haiku Contest Anthology, Leanfrog, Mainichi Haiku Contest Anthology, Mayfly, Midwest Haiku Anthology* (Brooks Books, 1992), *Modern Haiku, Muse-Pie, New Cicada, Northeast, Northwest Literary Forum, Outch, PEN Women 1998 International Poetry Contest, Persimmon, Plainsong, Plainspeak, Portals, Raw Nervz Haiku, Third Coast Archives, Tundra, Uguisu, Unaka Range, Uzzano, Wind Chimes, The Windless Orchard,* and *Woodnotes.*

Design and typography by Michael Dylan Welch.
Text set in 11/15 and 12/17 Sans Light Extended
with 14/18 and 26/30 Gill Sans Ultra Bold.

Preface

Randy Brooks is the prototypical Midwesterner—honest, cheerful, resourceful, hard-working, a loving husband, a doting father, and, above all, aware of and loyal to the past. These are characteristics that only someone with long roots in America's heartland could effortlessly possess. Integrity and energy emanate from the man, and, not surprisingly, from his haiku as well.

Brooks' earliest ancestors were farmers in Kansas and he and his family lived for a number of years on a farm in Indiana. This background explains why Brooks has written some of the most authentic farm-life haiku in the North American canon:

> snowblind on the range:
> homesteader feels
> the barbwire home

But rural haiku do not dominate this collection of over two-hundred poems, for Brooks, a professor at Millikin University in Decatur, Illinois, has become a city person, more comfortable with computers than with combines. Yet, growing up on farms has left him with nature-image–laden neurons from which he can draw connections that are as fresh as water from a spring.

While a sense of our vulnerability among powerful natural forces pervades the collection, the largest number of poems center, mostly in a joyful manner and frequently with humor, around sexuality, marriage, family, and children.

Few poets can catch the poignant as well as the inevitable funny moments that arise from intimacy:

> dawn after the birth,
> he brings her
> the first strawberry

And, I know of no haiku poet who has succeeded more in depicting the joys and the fears of being a child:

> up late with old friends . . .
> my daughter and her blankie
> out of the dark again

While Brooks is a first-rate observer of life in the Midwest, he is also capable of rendering the moments of awe and wonder that occur while on visits to very different and distant places—something not easy to do:

> open-mouthed
> behind museum glass,
>   samurai's war cry mask

When all is said and done, however, the most lasting impression is Brooks' powerful sense of legacy. Like the pull of gravity it keeps him constantly in touch with that most difficult of realizations—that we are indeed mortal:

she couldn't forgive
what she couldn't forgive—
grave sunken in

However, Brooks possesses a well-functioning third
eye—the artist's necessary detachment—and is fully
aware of the complexity of context and the possibility of
different perspectives.

As a result, he can find ways of seeing our mortality
that are less depressing than they are invigorating:

estate auction—
can't get my hand back out
of the cookie jar

School's Out is precisely what a selected works should
be: a showcase of a substantial number of haiku from
decades of work. It is a landmark collection and confirms
that Randy Brooks is one of the foremost haiku poets in
the English language.

George Swede
Toronto, Ontario

Author's Introduction

The title of this collection is *School's Out* for several reasons. First, when I reviewed the haiku I have written and that have been published since 1976, I noticed that a large majority of the poems are summer haiku. Perhaps this is simply the result of having time, as a teacher, to get outdoors and enjoy nature more in the summer. Or perhaps it is the result of a shift in brain activity. When school is out, I get to step down from my analytical frame of mind as a professor, and spend more time in a reflective or meditative state of mind that is more conducive to writing haiku.

A second reason for the title is that I believe in life-long learning, which extends beyond lessons in a classroom. Although I have never disliked school and have learned a great deal in school, I know that I have learned much when I have been "out of school" as well. I will always advocate summer vacations and sabbaticals because these are times when students and teachers can reconnect to the world, to life beyond the classroom, to nature. Haiku has taken me out into the woods, to the pond's edge, the shore line, the mountain ridge, the distant country, and haiku demanded that I learn from my observations, my perceptions, my feelings of being "out there."

The haiku tradition has called me to participate in the life of other beings, to understand the pine from the pine, to learn from nature rather than to impose my human nature onto nature. I admit that the teacher in my head has a hard time shutting up the constant analysis of life, but sometimes nature hushes me into that state of receptivity and being that results in a haiku from nature instead of from me. Some things you just can't learn from school; they are learned from life.

My haiku studies have always been after school, extra-curricular activities—the things I love to do when school's out. So the third reason for the title is that my most important teachers of haiku have come from beyond the requirements and electives of formal education. My teachers in school inspired me with a love of poetry and exposed me to Japanese literature, but my teachers beyond school courses were fellow writers in the haiku community, haiku editors, and translators of haiku. My first haiku mentor, Father Raymond Roseliep, wrote beautiful letters of encouragement and no-holds-barred criticism of a majority of my early haiku attempts.

In more recent years, my good friend, Lee Gurga, has met with me monthly to exchange responses and suggestions about our haiku. And of course, editors such as Robert Spiess, Cor van den Heuvel, William J. Higginson and translators including R. H. Blyth, Harold Henderson, Lucien Stryk, and Makoto Ueda have provided me with excellent opportunities for self-instruction through their haiku publications.

In the 1990s I have begun to receive academic recognition and support for my work in haiku, and I am now teaching courses on haiku at Millikin University. I wish to thank the university for providing me time (a sabbatical) and financial assistance in the form of faculty grants that have been invaluable in my own writing and studies of haiku. In May of 1998, I was named the Hardy Distinguished Professor of English. This honorary position includes significant institutional support for my continuing study of haiku as a global genre of literature. With great joy, I now bring my love of haiku to school, with the hope that my students find something of lasting value in the haiku reading and writing process. It is my hope that students will keep discovering the possibilities of writing and studying haiku as a creative process that will continue long after *School's Out*.

Randy M. Brooks
Millikin University
Decatur, Illinois

To Shirley

school's out—
a boy follows his dog
into the woods

circle in the dirt . . .
shadow of a thundercloud
stops the shooter

pumpkin pie aroma
from the back seat—
Kansas sunrise ahead

evening feeding—
old farmer's frosted breath
out to his cows

flag on the coffin . . .
    her gloves off to hold
        the child's hand tight

beside the chicken house
a cantaloupe skin
pecked clean

dirt farmer's wife
at the screen door—
no tractor sound

coyote howl
answered in the darkness:
face at the window

he opens his cupped palm . . .
a small tadpole with
a little wiggle left

grandpa
candles the egg—
"here son, see?"

door left open . . .
there he goes
with his kite

gramma hoes the beans
a weed clings
to her nylon anklet

show me yours.
you first.
barn roof creaks

no leaves
just the skeleton of a kite
in the uppermost branch

sisters bent over
the heating vent . . .
adult talk below

in the saddle,
grandpa straightens
his stooped shoulders

a farm kid wallows
in the rain pool:
the cattle wait

weathered ranch gate . . .
sunrise over
the row of blue spruce

snowblind on the range:
homesteader feels
the barbwire home

two lines in the water . . .
not a word between
father and son

no crumbs left,
the girl continues to reach
a carp's open mouth

rain . . .
bicyclist's hand out
from under the bridge

home from school,
he opens his lunch box

minnows

at the mailbox
the postman's dust
passes him

sand hill plums
farmers and their wives
in the creekbed

last day of school . . .
    the crack of a baseball bat
        outside the open window

swimming pool . . .
    a farm kid's arms pale
    from the elbows up

late afternoon . . .
all the cattle lie
in the billboard's shade

sun going down—
the bean-walkers shuffle
to the truck

farmyard girl's
apron full of eggs . . .
a curl dangles loose

barefoot along
the levee's sandy crest . . .
blackberry fingers

first kiss
deep in the woods . . .
sunbeams filter down

bullfrog eyes . . .
another daisy petal alights
on the surface

mare's road apples—
flaring to the scent,
the mustang's lips

freckle-face grin . . .
apple blossom
caught in her hair

pinetree trimmings—
mating luna moths
fumble to the ground

end of summer—
mountain wildflower
pressed in her diary

neon light flickers
on a crumpled beer can—
yellow jacket at the hole

factory shift change . . .
motorcycle wind lengthens
her strawberry hair

she reaches the morel—
a tendril of hair
caught on a thorn

toes dangle in the lake . . .
watermelon juice
drips off his chin

shady side of the lake—
snake tonguing its way
through tangled roots

blackberry pie
steaming on the window sill
blue morning moon

Sunday after lunch . . .
the secret of her pregnancy
on each sister's face

river to the edge
of the country road . . .
a little ripples over

the bride's mouth
stuffed with cake . . . the groom
answers for her

coconut cream pie—
the birthday candle
starts to slant

muskrat whiskers
twitch out of the water—
lightning illumines the shore

more summer rain . . .
an origami stork appears
on her fingertips

all three pregnant around
the kitchen table
slicing cantaloupe

in Lamaze class
her belly skin knots up . . .
gentle rain

full moon
over harvested fields—
her water breaks

mother & child
lie in bed—
rosebud on her breast

dawn after the birth,
he brings her
the first strawberry

rain at the window—
the newborn's fingers
catch in my beard

mice in the walls
      gentle rainfall
   on the roof

cooing for breath
as he nurses . . .
snow drips from the oak

windshield wipers
smear the freezing rain . . .
the sick baby's muffled cry

minister's hand
over the baby's soft spot—
she hushes

snap of her bra . . .
the baby stops crying
to open his mouth

the baby's curl
straightened with a comb . . .
bath drain gurgles

high as my arms
can lift him . . .
the moon still out of reach

whitewater's lullaby—
the baby asleep
on my lap

top stair creaks—
the baby's fingers part
then settle back to sleep

my sister cups her hands . . .
how the nurse showed her
the miscarried fetus

the leaf shadows
on the kitchen floor—
baby talks to herself

cherry buckets full . . .
a pair of jenny wrens
scold us from the fence

black ants
from under the refrigerator . . .
the toddler lifts one foot

bath towel
around her headache . . .
frost ferns up the window

face
in the window—
no moon

ghost town cemetery—
five family names
and the Kansas wind

a muledeer
hunkers down in the wheat—
the combine stops

the pinwheel stops
grandpa catches
his breath

all tongue
the clam in the fire's
hiss

looking over her shoulder,
the waves come in
one more time

whispers
over the telephone—
the widow's cancer

maple seeds spiraling—
cicada husk holds on
to the old swing rope

sculpture garden . . .
the marble bench
cool through my jeans

heat clicks
on
the wavering fern

pair of robins
in the tall grass . . .
my daughter's swing slows

poking his cane
into the mud—
corn not planted yet

one pawn missing . . .
sunburst through an opening
in the thunderhead

her newest folksong—
warmth of fireplace coals
through the screen

middle of the night
    my pregnant wife leaves me
    cool crumpled sheets

full moon
through the kitchen window—
two aspirins in my palm

lights out
I follow the sound
to my wife's breathing

Thanksgiving sunrise . . .
cheesecloth over the rolls
in the back seat window

riding down
    the metro escalator,
        snowflakes

stockings on the mantle . . .
the child's eyes follow sparks
up the chimney

Christmas morning—
 misty breath of cows
 rising where they lie

furrows of water
mirror the gray sky . . .
farmer at the closed gate

tennis shoes held high—
flood water swirls
around her thighs

his vomit wiped up . . .
my bowl of wheaties
soggy now

the Art Institute—
bronze lion's tail
dripping autumn rain

each stroke of the crayon
his tongue
across his lips

load of seedwheat—
pumping old brakes
all the way down the hill

fallen apple
rolls into the pile of leaves . . .
yellow jacket rights itself

autumn chill . . .
we scootch our lawnchairs
closer to the grill

praising the hostess,
eggnog
in his moustache

toddler's finger
touches the surface . . .
out of the depths, a goldfish

dawn rain
dripping off autumn leaves
her yawn   my yawn

reflections of masts
rippling in the bay . . .
        the grebe pops under

the dark white sand
pocked with raindrops . . .
our tracks the only ones

home from the funeral
hands in the dishwater suds
sister-to-sister

grandpa's grave on the prairie . . .
snowflakes caught behind
each clod of dirt

estate auction—
can't get my hand back out
of the cookie jar

Amish lady . . .
only her warm smile
makes up her face

a shiny disco shirt
out of the attic trunk . . .
something scurries away

black panties—
she lifts one leg,
then an eyebrow

snow halfway up
all the windows . . .
   the cat in heat

grandpa's cedar cane
  my son poking holes
  in a snow drift

Heimliched out of me
pink candy heart
wordless now

toddler stands
on the old cat's senseless tail . . .
sun soaking in

Easter lily
on the shut-in's coffee table . . .
fingers over each petal

old calico
comes in from the garage—
  cobweb whiskers

  she couldn't forgive
  what she couldn't forgive—
  grave sunken in

sawing—
the sap begins to flow
out of this evergreen

spring afternoon . . .
I try another combination
on the shed lock

shutters thrown open
a fly
straight in

big brother's grin . . .
the last piece of the puzzle
out of his pocket

Mom's sunburnt back . . .
first the youngest touches it,
then the eldest

low tide . . .
    here comes the sunrise lady
    with her paper bag

her leg
swinging, swinging:
the test still incomplete

one leg over the oar,
    the college graduate
        drifts

holding hands . . .
until we reach
the blackberries

new grave . . .
a graduation tassel
hangs from the stone

the daughter taps flour
into a mixing bowl . . .
mother's apron tight

cedar walking cane
hangs from the coat rack
dust on the handle's curve

through the open door . . .
her smile doesn't forgive
all my sins

police lights—
the body in the street,
a yellow tabby

eyeing the spot
where our bumpers bumped—
snow in his thick eyebrows

coffee shop . . .
the only empty seat
still warm

faintly through
the airport's noise—
   distant bugle taps

up late with old friends . . .
my daughter and her blankie
out of the dark again

wind in the leaves—
Santōka's begging bowl
in a glass case

cool haiku stone . . .
black ant down and out
of the kanji

sundown . . .
fish bubble the water
after fallen mayflies

stepping stones
to the garden tea house . . .
pockets of morning rain

pair of sunken boats
in the Japanese garden . . .
green tea

evening cool . . .
only the widow's muddied shoes
on the back porch

plumes of pampas grass
wavering in the plaza . . .
the poet's toupee askew

mourning dove
returns to the porch rail
new snow fluffs off

the lift
of the crow's feet
downing on a branch

dusty screen door . . .
the widow's bent-tailed cat
sniffs the spring rain

unable to find
desire within herself . . .
the treetop cardinal calls

potato planting . . .
the old woman's song
the rhythm of her hoe

scooping a handful
of mountaintop snowmelt . . .
her face a child's

yesterday
we laid her in the ground;
peach blossoms

persimmons hang
in the leafless tree:
street leaves skitter

we walk through
the empty farm house—
her eyes well up

mockingbird song—
family cat too old to shake
dew off her paw

cool river canyon . . .
magpie's cry as I hammer in
the tent spike

heat of the afternoon—
two horses on the cliff
face the wind

mellow thunder . . .
I slip off my sandals
to feel the cool

after all these years
she asks about her mother . . .
I put on another log

our teenagers
on the whitewater raft . . .
I let go of the rope

fingers feel the letters
of her name . . .
wisteria over the tombstone

garage sale . . .
the halter top she wore
on our honeymoon

suitcases against the car
first sprinkles of rain
on my eyeglasses

horsefly kicking
in the pond water . . .
a bubble from below

aspen leaves
shimmer over the riverbank—
hummingbird hovers

ticking
the fishing line in . . .
    sunrise through the pines

warm rocks
along the mountain stream . . .
snake's tongue, a flick of blue

old cowpath . . .
    the killdeer
    fakes a broken wing

open-mouthed
behind museum glass,
    samurai's war cry mask

a small cricket
across the chancel carpet . . .
elder's prayer goes on and on

stewardship Sunday . . .
   the old woman's hand shakes
   the offering plate

bingo boards empty—
   another widow intercepts
   the old man's wink

her mother's cat
now dead, too . . .
frost on the tomatoes

frost in the garden . . .
tucking the cat's feet in
with my spade

cemetery cuttings . . .
tulips her mother planted
along the white pickets

long drive home . . .
our talk of the past goes
into the future

fountain off . . .
    autumn rain darkens
    the stone faces

funeral procession . . .
snowflakes blowing
into the headlights

first
snow

no
walk
long
enough

About the Author

Randy M. Brooks was born in Hutchinson, Kansas, on June 18, 1954. He grew up in western Kansas where his ancestors were homesteaders, teachers, and farmers. He studied American literature and philosophy at Ball State University in Muncie, Indiana, receiving a B.A. with honors in 1975. In 1977, he completed an M.A. in American literature and linguistics from Purdue University in West Lafayette, Indiana, and after several years of working in the library, he earned his Ph.D. in rhetoric and technical writing from Purdue University in 1990. He is an associate professor of English at Millikin University where he directs the writing major. He lives with his wife and three children in Decatur, Illinois.

In 1976 Randy Brooks founded High/Coo Press and launched *High/Coo: A Quarterly of Short Poetry* with his wife, Shirley. In that same year, they started publishing chapbooks of haiku and short poetry, beginning with Raymond Roseliep's *Sun in His Belly* as the first in the series. A year later they instituted an annual mini-chapbook competition featuring small thematic or sequential collections of haiku in English. From 1980 until 1988, they published *Haiku Review*, a bibliography of haiku publications and criticism that featured an ongoing review of recent haiku books by Elizabeth Searle Lamb.

When they moved to Illinois, Randy and Shirley renamed the publishing company Brooks Books, and they currently publish clothbound books, chapbooks, and a small haiku magazine called *Mayfly*. Their catalog lists forty-eight haiku titles in print. The Brooks also publish the "English-Language Haiku Web Site," started in the spring of 1998 as a means of featuring English-language haiku poets and books.

In 1998 and 1999 Randy Brooks teamed up with George Swede to edit *Global Haiku: 25 Outstanding Poets* (Iron Press, forthcoming). And in 1992 he teamed up with Lee Gurga as co-editor of the *Midwest Haiku Anthology*, which received second place in the 1993 Haiku Society of America Merit Book Awards. In 1996 they teamed up as editors of *A Solitary Leaf: Haiku Society of America 1996 Members Anthology.*

Dr. Brooks has received numerous awards for his haiku and several grants for academic studies of haiku. He frequently shares his interest in haiku through public readings, presentations, and workshops for all ages.

Award Credits

"dirt farmer's wife" (page 20) — Editor's Personal Favorite Award, *Modern Haiku*, February 1977

"door left open . . ." (page 22) — Honorable Mention, 1988 Japan Airlines Haiku Contest

"two lines in the water . . ." (page 26) — Best of Issue, *Modern Haiku* XXIX:2, Winter/Spring 1998

"no crumbs left" (page 27) — Third Place, Kumamoto International Kusamakura Haiku Competition, Japan, 1998

"face" (page 51) — Bonsai Quarterly Award, *Bonsai Quarterly*, January 1977

"cool haiku stone . . ." (page 82) — Castle Post Haiku Award, Matsuyama Castle, Japan, 1998, and Matsuyama Tourism Haiku Award sponsored by the Shiki Haiku Museum and the city of Matsuyama, Japan, July 1997

"pair of sunken boats" (page 83) — Honorable Mention, PEN Women 1998 International Poetry Contest, Palomar, California, April 1998

"after all these years" (page 91) — Haiku Competition Award, *Mainichi Daily News*, Tokyo, 1997

"funeral procession" (page 99) — Harold G. Henderson Award, Haiku Society of America, 1998